Table of Contents:

ARE YOU READY?

INTRODUCTION:
I'VE NEVER DONE THIS BEFORE

If you're like most people, at some point you've had an idea that caused you to create a plan. You then spent numerous hours creating, adjusting, and dreaming of what that idea will bring. Eventually, something gets in the way and nothing ever happens, or worse yet, someone else beats you to the punch. In this book, you will learn my secret formula to turn those ideas into a reality. The best part is, it's easier than you ever imagined.

Don't believe me? Good, because I have a surprise. The book that you are about to read is being written using the exact formula the book is actually about. The formula, further referenced as the Do Things Method™, will be the subject of this book and the method by which it is created. Let me try and explain this a little more clearly. To start, I had an idea about writing a book to share the Do Things Method™ with the world. It would be easy for that idea to simply stay in my brain as I learn "how" to write a book. Seeing that I have no experience or knowledge of how the book writing or publishing process works, I could easily have that be the very reason not to take action. This huge unknown is quite honestly exactly why people never succeed in what they set out to accomplish. I've never written, designed, or published a book. Literally, this is starting from zero with an idea and taking it all the way to reality. If I have no experience or real understanding of what I'm getting into and still end up with an actual finished book to distribute, the theoretical formula will be proven by the same medium in which it is explained. Does that make sense? Sounds very "meta" to me and that's why I think I like this concept so much.

Hopefully, the fact that I'm practicing what I preach will also give you a greater feeling of confidence and encouragement to use the Do Things Method™ the next time you have an idea that could potentially change your life or the lives of people around you. My passion is to share my experience and insight with as many people as possible so that they, in turn, will be able to live their lives to the full potential they were created to reach. You'll hear me say this again, but YOU are a MIRACLE created by God to do AMAZING things. Sometimes, we need a little kick in the butt to realize that...or an enormous smack across the face. Whichever one you need, it is my prayer that this book can be a catalyst for your action and get you on the path to accomplishing whatever your AMAZING things are.

Before we continue, there are a few things I would like to address. First, throughout this book you will read many personal stories that illustrate different phases of the Do Things Method™. The purpose of these stories is to give you a clear understanding of how each piece fits into our actual lives and is not simply a theoretical philosophy intended to sell a utopian idea that has no basis in reality.

Second, I will reference stories from the Bible. Now, I don't know what your position is on the Bible or what you have or have not read of it. For me, the Bible has been an integral part of my life and is the basis for my worldview. It is important to note that from a factual standpoint, the Bible is a collection of writings from real people, in real places, at real times. Some of the accounts are historical in nature and others are artistic expressions intended to help communicate an eternal idea to be understood by our finite minds. If you have further questions or concerns related to what is in the Bible, I would encourage you to read it for yourself, research its origins, and decide how you interpret the writings. Throughout my life, I have found the Bible to be true and complete. My prayer is that as you read this book and gain an understanding of the Do Things Method™ and how it can change your approach to life, it may also encourage you to revisit any previous thoughts or feelings about the writings found in the Bible.

Next, this book is NOT an excuse to take obviously wrong or hurtful action involving any other person, place or thing. It is not an excuse to go against common sense or justification for intended harm. Granted, this book is encouraging you to take action that may take you in a direction unpopular with the people around you, but the intent of your action should be in an effort to live the adventure you were meant to live not to purposely disrupt the adventures of others. Simply put, assume this method is only to be used for good, not adapted by the dark side.

Also, because the intent of this book is to get people to stop over thinking and start doing, it is not very long. In fact, I've tried to abbreviate the stories as much as possible to make sure only the important pieces remain so that we don't spend endless hours on miniscule details that do not push us towards action. Hopefully you appreciate the brevity and directness of the writing. For me, reading is not a leisure activity. If there is something I need to know, I read it, or listen to it if I can, then move on and start implementing.

Finally, this book is a work of passion that has come from personal experience with an intent to help you in this adventure called life. When I say, "YOU are a MIRACLE" I mean it...even if we have dissimilar world views. It is my belief that through reading this book, you will find that, regardless of any difference you and I may have, our common human goal is the same. We all want to live the life we were meant to live. It is my opinion that this journey starts with a mindset, followed by action, and completed by doing those two steps continually, making slight adjustments with each revolution.

SO, WHAT'S THE PLAN?

CHAPTER 1

BURN YOUR PLANS™

Every year for the past six years our family of five has taken a trip to get out of town after my busy season at the office. We've done everything from exploring San Francisco for a week to staying two nights at a local hotel. Anything we can do to get away and connect for some extended amount of time is always the goal. This past year, when we started planning for the coming trip, we decided another road trip was in order. We felt it was time to venture out of our great state of California to the Grand Canyon and see some natural American beauty. Now to be fair, we aren't big planners to begin with. Typically, these vacations are "planned" only a few months before the day we leave. That may give some of you anxiety already but wait, it gets worse. Uniquely, this year was the first full year we had been homeschooling our kids so we really had as much time to go on our excursion as my work schedule would allow. Being self employed that really meant, "How long can we be away from home before my business can't stay afloat?" It was an opportunity to plan a trip that would have never been accomplished in previous years.

In late February, we were hanging out with some friends of ours. They were telling us about their plans to drive up the coast of California into Canada and be gone for the entire summer. What an adventure! Imagine the things they would see. Think of the people they would meet. It would be the trip of a lifetime.

After they left that night, Tammy and I looked at each other. We both wondered what the other was thinking. It turns out, we were both thinking the same thing. "Why couldn't WE do an epic road trip for the entire summer?" As we sat down to briefly talk through the details of this idea, it became abundantly clear that we had started the planning process a little too late.

After all, a trip of this magnitude would need months or maybe even years of planning to be sure it was a success, right? Did that stop us? Not at all. We thought this feeling of uncertainty mixed with a strong call to take action may have been a fraction of what Noah felt when God asked him to build an Ark. If Noah could build an Ark, we could take an epic road trip for the entire summer.

At the time, the lease for our home was ending and we had yet to sign a new agreement which meant we could do something REALLY drastic. It was scary drastic. What if we ended our lease, sold most of our possessions, bought an RV and stayed out on the road as long as possible? That night we went to bed with the idea of taking the most epic vacation we had ever been on. Here's where the issues started to arise. First, would I be able to work enough on the road to pay for our entire adventure? Second, where could we find an RV on short notice to take on our trip? Third, what would our kids think about this idea? The list continued. Oh, and probably the most realistic reason for us not to leave for an unspecified amount of time in an RV with very little resources….I've NEVER driven an RV before.

The following week was full of conversations and research. Using the internet and reaching out to some friends we knew who had taken trips similar to this before, we gathered as much information as we could. Most of the people we discussed our potential plans with expressed numerous concerns and asked multiple questions that we simply couldn't answer. At the end of that week, we had made our decision. Our family of five was going to set out on an adventure of a lifetime whether we were ready or not.

By this time, it was early March and we needed to make some quick decisions, inform our landlord of the plans, and get prepared for the unknown. Within that week, we found and purchased an RV, gutted our house, and started lining up the details of the trip. Did I mention that I'd never driven an RV before? Well, that ended up making an impact in our itinerary...literally.

The day we purchased the RV, that I had still never driven up to that point, we had to drive it from San Diego, CA 100 miles all the way back to our home in Orange County, CA. To make things even more stressful, it was 5:00pm which is perfect timing for rush hour traffic on one of the busiest stretches of freeway in Southern California. Are you nervous for us yet?

Prior to driving the 100 miles home, I had only driven the 40' diesel pusher for about 10 miles with the previous owner to learn the ins and outs of the vehicle. Long story short, we made it home with no issues. What a relief! Our first hurdle had been completed. When we returned home, it was late and the kids needed to go to bed. Tammy said to me, "Wait here. I'll go put the kids to bed and then I'll help you back it into the side yard for the night." I of course agreed, said goodnight to the kids and watched her go inside. As I sat there in our new beast of a recreational vehicle, I had a thought. "If I was able to drive this thing 100 miles safely home, than I can easily back it in for the night by myself."

If you've already figured it out, that thought didn't remain just a thought. I started up the grumbling diesel engine and began to put the RV away for the night. By myself. Did I mention it was night time and dark? It wasn't long before something didn't feel right and I suddenly heard a loud scraping sound and then a thunderous "SLAM". As I pulled forward to reposition myself. Tammy came running out of the house. "What did you do?" she exclaimed. When I exited the vehicle, and looked outside, I could see that I had missed my mark by much further than I had anticipated. The corner of the roof found a way to puncture the back end of our ginormous motor coach. "How did that happen?" I thought. It turns out that attempting to park a 40' recreational vehicle in a side yard at night for the very first time by yourself was NOT a good idea. I had managed to back the RV into the house that we were just getting ready to leave. If you'd like to see more of this story, you can watch the videos on our YouTube channel. Yes, I turned on the camera to show the world that I had made a HUGE mistake.

When we reached out to our insurance company and finally got the RV into the repair shop, we were told the RV had $20,000 worth of damage but because we had insurance in place, it was going to cost us just over $1,000. The worst part was it would delay our trip by over four weeks. For many people, that may have been a sign to quit. A reason to change the plans. A reason to take a less risky path. Why would we do that? This was going to be the trip of a lifetime! We could wait a few weeks. So we did.

The details of that trip are so awesome that we've decided they deserve their own platform to share with you so I won't be getting into them all in this book. Some of the trip is posted in video form on our YouTube channel but there are so many things to share, it couldn't all be done here. After all, this book isn't about how the Frazier's took an 86 day road trip to 43 states and Canada. No! This is about the formula we used to step out in faith and attempt a trip that many of the people who knew we were leaving said they'd love to do but could never pull the trigger. This book is the secret to how we were able to have little to no plan and still take action and experience something few people ever will. It's been said many times before, "no risk, no reward" but how do we get ourselves to take a risk? Especially when there is no way in knowing what the results will be; when you can't plan for every detail or know what new hurdle will be around the corner.

What's the plan you may ask? I'll tell you. The plan is not a plan. The plan is action. That action, creates a plan. The plan today, won't be the plan tomorrow and the plan you start with will rarely be the steps that take you to success. For most of us, we get caught up in trying to devise the perfect plan. We diagram, list, draw, visualize, and articulate how we expect to reach a goal. Our expectation is that we can predictably control the outcomes of each step of our plan as we approach our goal. The reality is, we have NO control over most things. Ultimately, the only two things we ever have control over in life is first our effort and second, our perspective. That means that if we want to succeed amongst a sea of impossibility, we have to first get our minds right. We have to rely on faith. We have to believe that there is a purpose to our creation. To do that, we need to start by burning our plans.

PHASE 1

PERSPECTIVE

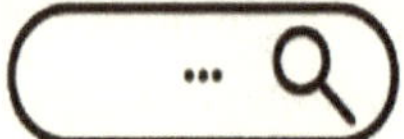

CHAPTER 2

YOU ARE A MIRACLE

We all have a purpose. I don't know where you stand on the meaning of life but I have a strong belief that we are all here for a purpose. Each of us was created with unique gifts and abilities by a Creator that desires us to reach the potential each of us has ingrained into who we are. Sadly, few of us ever have the opportunity to use those gifts or even discover what they may be. Many times the reason we fail to embrace or uncover these gifts is a matter of mindset; a lack of faith that we actually were created for a purpose. How we think about who we are is often times shaped by the opinions of people around us. That's where we get it wrong. We are spiritual beings created by a God that wants us to succeed, even though the people around us may not see it. Let me prove that, regardless of what anyone has ever said about you or to you, YOU are a MIRACLE created to do AMAZING things. It's true. If the spiritual aspect of what I'm saying isn't enough yet, let's try another approach. How about we use math? Let me explain.

The Harvard Law Review did a study related to the probability, from a mathematical and scientific perspective, that you and I exist on this planet. It's been said by many, prior to this study, that the probability was 1 in 400 trillion. That is a GINORMOUS number in itself. Which is enough for me to believe on logic alone that we are all miracles and created to do AMAZING things, but if that's not enough to convince you, let's see what the Harvard Law Review came up with. They started with the probability that a boy meets a girl and that same exact couple has a child. That worked out to be 1 in 40 million which is roughly the chances of winning the California Super Lotto Jackpot. Sounds pretty lucky to me. From there, they calculated the probability that a specific egg meets a specific sperm to create a specific life. That worked out to be 1 in 400 quadrillion. If you had 400 quadrillion pennies you would have over $10 trillion dollars. As if that isn't far enough, they went one step further to calculate the fact that you are a unique human that comes from a unique family tree. Now we're up to 1 in 10 with 2,685,000 zeros behind it. With all this science and math, it's safe to say that when you convert these calculations to a percentage there is a 0% chance that you even exist. What? You and I shouldn't even exist? Crazy, but it's true. Realistically even at 1 in 400 trillion, it works out to be around 0% as well.

Either way you look at the calculations, neither you, your family, friends, or strangers should even exist. If we can look at life with the shock and awe that comes with these calculations it is impossible to see our existence as anything other than a miracle. It follows that if we are a miracle, we are here for a reason. I believe that reason is to do amazing things.

When we have a new lense to look through when it comes to challenging or even seemingly impossible situations, I think things seem to feel much less overwhelming. Doing something that to outsiders seems impossible starts to feel a little more possible because, if we've beaten the odds of being alive, doing a little thing like starting a new job or saying hello to an attractive human being shouldn't be so scary. Most of the time we get disproportionately focused on the little things. Usually the things that, from a big picture standpoint, will never actually make a difference.

My family and I have participated in the Disneyland 5k run every September over the past five years. We rarely did any training to get prepared for the race but also never truly competed against any of the other racers. We simply ran the race as an exercise in promoting health as a family and sharing a fun experience together. Two years ago, I thought it might be fun to also participate in the half marathon. Now, I'm not a runner. I played football in college, which was over 10 years ago, and tried to exercise as little as possible ever since. Never the less, I thought, "How hard could it be? It's just over 13 miles and I've seen some of the people that run these races. I'll be fine. I'm not trying to part the Red Sea. It's just a little running." So with that perspective, I signed up for the half marathon race that year. We changed nothing in preparation for the race even though this would be the longest race I'd ever run and technically the longest I'd ever run period. The Friday before my half marathon was the 5k that we were running as a family. Seeing that with the two races over the weekend I would run a total of over 16 miles, it seemed logical to me that I should make sure and eat a big breakfast. As we entered the local Anaheim International House Of Pancakes, my mouth began to water while I pictured the large stack of fluffy cakes I was about to consume.

So, I was about to run farther than I had ever run in my life, did almost no training, and ate way too many pancakes in preparation for the weekend. Great plan, right? We ran the 5k with no issues. When we got through the finish line, it started to hit me that in less than 48 hours I would be running over four times that much. It dawned on me that I may have made a mistake. The morning of the race came and I reluctantly got out of bed. It was 5:00am and I don't usually wake up before 7:30am so needless to say, I was struggling. When I got to the starting line with the thousands of other people, I started to feel invigorated. "If all these people who don't seem to be Olympic runners can make it through this, then so can I." In the spirit of optimism, I decided that to make this experience even more memorable, I turned on my phone and went to my Facebook app, selected the "LIVE video" button and began to stream video of me from the starting line waiting for the race to start. It was still early so there weren't too many people watching yet but it struck a new idea for the race. "What if I try and live stream multiple times throughout the race to share this journey with others. It will either encourage others to get out of their comfort zone, or people may be entertained by the excruciating time I'm having after not preparing for the race and stuffing my face with tasty flapjacks the morning before." Both sounded like a win to me, so that was the plan.

By mile six, I had live streamed and interacted with people as I was running and actually received quite a bit of encouragement from the people watching. Ultimately, it turned into much more of a support for me than I had expected. When it got tough, I turned on the camera and someone on the other side of the stream commented something along the lines of "Keep going." or "You can do this." It was amazing. The people that I was interacting with were helping me finish the race.

Eventually, I got to the end of the race. It was hard. I was tired. Ultimately, I finished and that's all that mattered. That day I learned a very important lesson that strengthened my faith and ultimately my theory about everyone having a purpose. We all have struggles in life. Everyone gets stuck at some point no matter how perfect things may seem. When we have relationships and connect with people, we share a common bond. If we can lean into our humanity and share our difficulties, we can connect and lift each other up when we least expect it. That in itself is AMAZING.

There's a chance that when you read the part earlier that YOU are a MIRACLE and created by God to do AMAZING things, you interpreted the AMAZING things to be grand or extravagant. That's not what I mean. The word AMAZING is more than that. Doing something amazing looks different for everyone. It's related to our strengths and gifts that we have been blessed with. What do you have that makes you who you are? Sharing a smile with someone is amazing when it is exactly what they need. Caring for others and helping other people have a better life is definitely amazing. After all, the fact that we even exist is inconceivable. This life itself is a gift. Everything else is nothing short of amazing. When we look at the world like that, we can't help but be ready to take a leap of faith and do things.

CHAPTER 3

MEAN INTERNET LADY

Alright, so by this point if you're still reading I assume you at least are interested to see how changing your mindset about who you are will change your ability to have faith and do a thing before you have the perfect plan. That being said, there will be a lot of people that still don't agree. The great philosopher, Taylor Swift said it best in her song when she said, "Haters gonna hate." It's true. People will not always understand where you are going or why you are doing a thing. In the Bible, there is a story you may have heard about a young shepherd boy named David. David was ridiculed by the Israelites and Philistines for being nothing more than a shepherd. He then defied their protests and proceeded to sling a stone toward Goliath on the battlefield. It flew through the air and struck Goliath in the head and he dropped. That stone killed a giant. None of the Israelite warriors were confident enough to even face this beast of a man yet David, a boy with no encouragement from the people around him, stood up and took action. He let those "Haters Hate" and did a thing in spite of their ridicule.

My point is, you don't have to have other people's approval to take action. Did you know that? Other people don't control your actions. You have the authority to do whatever you want. Now, that doesn't mean that there aren't consequences for the things you do. If you choose to take a negative action against someone, there will be repercussions. If you choose to break a law, there most likely will be punishment. That still doesn't change the fact that you have the choice to act or not to act. It really is that simple even though sometimes you may not feel that way.

When was the last time the words or actions from someone actually stopped you from doing something? I don't mean the last time you chose not to take action because of what someone else said or did, but when it was actually impossible for you to take action? For most of us, the answer is never. We do, however, frame things in our minds based on what other people say or do that cause us to choose not to take action. It's that result that I want to address in this chapter. You have a choice, no matter what the outside world says or does. That doesn't mean it's easy to ignore the haters and do a thing. It doesn't feel good to share an idea with a family member and have them tell you all the things wrong with that idea; especially when we value the opinion of someone that maybe doesn't understand our perspective. However, if we can focus on our miracle status, look past those thoughts and feelings to take action, we can truly start to recognize our potential and learn what amazing things we were created to do.

Now, this may surprise some of you but, I LOVE the internet! Seriously, it's SO great. You can find almost anything or anyone in an instant. Yes, I understand that there is a realistic concern about how that can be used as a tool for evil. In most cases though, it is simply a tool to connect us in a way we have never been able to do before. Something that I've been doing for quite some time now is posting videos to places like Facebook, Instagram, and YouTube. It's fun for me and I get to spread my message of love, action, and positivity to exponentially more people by using the internet. For many people, posting content online can be extremely scary. The fear of other people's reaction to your post will stop quite a few of us from sharing even the simplest of messages. We cannot let that stop us.

It wasn't long ago that I started posting videos with a serious intent to help motivate people to "DO THINGS" and live their purpose. One of the very first videos I posted was called "MIRACLE" and it was a somewhat artsy type of video that was a little out of my comfort zone. During the edit, I made multiple changes and adjustments to make sure the message was just right. This video was going to be great! I couldn't wait to get it online and start seeing people's reaction to this message.

It was late one night when I uploaded the video. Since I felt it was an extremely important and valuable video, I decided to run a promotion with it in an attempt to reach more people. If you don't know what that means, I made it a paid promotional video on Facebook to put it in front of people that weren't already connected to my page. When I woke up the next morning, I went straight to my computer to check and see how the video had done overnight. Wow! Over 2,000 views and 35 comments! It was awesome.

As I read through the comments with feedback from people that had connected with the message, one comment stood out. It didn't fit with the theme of the rest of the feedback I had received. It wasn't positive. As a matter of fact, it wasn't even about the message. "What?" I thought to myself. Here is the comment I received,

"HA! You're drinking STARBUCKS coffee. That means you can't be trusted and I'll NEVER watch your videos again."

-Mean Internet Lady

What in the world was this? Was she serious? Did she watch this video and miss the ENTIRE point?

My immediate response was to reply to her comment in a way that I'm sure wouldn't help promote my message of love, action, and positivity. You probably have a few ideas of what those comments could have been. I'll let you use your imagination to think of how I WANTED to reply. After a while, I was able to calm down and look at this comment with a little different perspective. Why did she focus on the three seconds of my drinking out of a coffee cup, with no logo on it, and feel the need to comment with such negativity? It made me start to feel bad for her. She was angry. Maybe she had a bad experience at Starbucks? Whatever the reason, Mean Internet Lady needed some help. That was my que. I sat down and replied to her comment,

"Wow, you must love coffee! It's nice that we have something in common. Have an amazing day and remember, you're a MIRACLE!"

We all have had similar situations with people that responded to our actions in a way that didn't reflect the intent of what we were doing. The response felt like it came out of nowhere and we retreated or responded poorly to them. I'm sure this comment isn't the worst you've seen. Maybe it's not even the worst you've done when reacting to someone else's actions. The point is, we all have different perspectives. Each of us sees the world differently. If you have a vision for something, there is someone out there that can poke holes in it or tell you why it's a bad idea. That is just a fact. The reality is we need to understand that, hear what others have to say, decide whether or not their response has any value for us, and then move on. Have faith in the purpose for your actions. We cannot let others direct our path when they may or may not understand our vision. Doing things that make progress towards our ultimate goal is the plan, even when Mean Internet Lady gives us her unwanted and unguided response. Like Taylor said, "haters gonna hate". Let them. Put that stone in your pocket and walk towards the giant. In the end, they may be the ones most impacted by your success. However, if you never act, there is absolutely no chance that you will reach your potential, impact anybody, or live the life you were created to live.

Oh, you can go watch my "coffee video" on YouTube, Facebook, or my website FrazierMethod.com if you'd like to see why I can't be trusted. Haha. Ok, I'm done. Moving on.

CHAPTER 4

YOU CAN'T CONTROL CHRISTMAS

There is an undeniable fact that must be understood. Christmas is the absolute best time of year. Baby Jesus' birthday, music, lights, jolly holiday parties, and the presents. If you don't like Christmas, I'll pray for you. Seriously though, Christmas is my favorite time of year. It always has been.

One year in particular, I started uncharacteristically early planning my list for Santa. Did you make lists? Each year, my brother and I would sit and talk about the things we had seen in the stores or in the SEARS catalog. Yes, I'm old. This year was a different year. I had a plan, and it started with the list.

For some reason, this year there were a larger than normal number of items that I was anticipating opening on Christmas morning. As I started compiling my list, it became apparent that I needed a system. I needed a way to communicate the importance of each item on the list to make sure the big man knew the order in which to get them for me. Suddenly it came to me. I grabbed a new sheet of paper and a crayon. Starting at the top with the BIGGEST priority on the list. A puppy. We had a dog before and she was the best. After she died, we didn't have a new dog for a while and I was ready to have a pet again. So at the top of my carefully curated list I wrote in big bold letters,

1.   **PUPPY**

It was perfect. The list started there and went all the way down to #50 - Cowboy Hat. To answer your question, yes, I was a selfish kid. Weren't we all though? Anyway, as the days slipped away and Christmas got closer, I made sure to do all the right things. I was kind to my brother. I did all my chores and homework. I sent letters to the North Pole. I even prayed for God to make sure I got all the things on my list. The plan was foolproof. I was in control, or at least I thought I was.

On Christmas Eve I could barely sleep. It was going to be the BEST Christmas morning EVER! Christmas morning came and it was go time. My brother and I sprinted to the tree with unbridled anticipation. Our Christmas pajamas could barely keep up with us.

When we got to the family room and looked at what was under the tree, I started to feel a little confused. We didn't hear any barking or scratching coming from any box. There was no sign of a puppy anywhere! "That's fine." I thought. "Maybe it wouldn't stay in the box and is outside somewhere. Ooh! Or maybe it's just hidden somewhere so we are surprised." My mind kept reeling but I played it cool on the outside.

As we started opening the presents, it was becoming apparent that someone hadn't received my list. Yes, there were some things from my list but they didn't follow the protocol set forth by the list and worst of all, there was still no puppy! It was getting late in the morning and we had opened all of the presents. No puppy. No Cowboy hat. What happened? Where did I go wrong? It didn't make sense. I had a foolproof plan. I did all the right things. Why couldn't I control Christmas?

That Christmas I learned a valuable lesson. You can't control Christmas. You can't control much of anything, really. The truth is, you can only actually control two things. The first thing you have control over is your mindset. Your perspective. How you see the world and what you think about it is completely under your control. That is why the Do Things Method™ starts with PERSPECTIVE. There is no way to control what other people think. There is no way to control what other people say or do. There is no way to control your external circumstances. You can however, control how you view all of those things. If you can have a renewed perspective about what's happening around you, it makes the next area of control extremely more impactful. Remember to focus on your miracle status. No matter what happens, that can never be taken from you. The next area we can control is our actions. What we do. What we say. How we react to the things we can't control is what we absolutely do have control over.

No matter how great your plans are or how amazing your expectations may be, you don't have control of the things that may happen to directly impact those plans. This is exactly why the Do Things Method™ exists. It's all about having faith in your purpose and staying focused on what you can control. It is not about spending time on the things you can't. You don't need a complete plan. You barely even need a second step. All you need is a little faith and a direction.

CHAPTER 5

LET'S GO EAST

When I first tell someone about the Do Things Method™ their initial question is, "so, what is it?" Then I tell them it's about taking action and doing things. Next they fire back with, "So, like just do anything? Shouldn't it be about doing the 'right' thing?" To which I reply, "What is the 'right' thing?" This typically gets a multitude of different responses but ultimately, the answer is in the question. If you follow my logic that your action creates the plan, but you have no plan, then how do you know the "right" thing to do? Ah, now we're getting somewhere. The next step in the PERSPECTIVE part of the Do Things Method™ addresses this issue.

When we started this conversation, I said, "If you're like most people, at some point you've had an idea that caused you to create a plan." Once you've understood that you are a MIRACLE, and that "Mean Internet Lady" has her own issues that shouldn't affect your decision to act, and you can only control your perspective and effort, it's time to talk about that idea which started this whole ball rolling. The idea is what we look at next. No matter what the idea is, how big or how small, how complicated or simple, this "idea" has a direction. There is some place you are attempting to go. In a sense, this direction is the extent of your "plan". Yes, I said to burn your plans but you need to hold on to your direction. If it makes you feel better, you can call this direction your "plan". The reality is that you can call it whatever you want, just don't spend more time on it than using it as a compass to start taking action.

At this point you might be thinking, "Todd, I'm confused. How is this about doing the RIGHT thing?" Understood, let's get to that. Once we've established the direction we are heading, it's time to start moving that way. However, we all have free will. We have the ability to choose. We can't control anything other than OUR perspective and OUR effort. So, be intentional about your action. If your idea is intended to harm someone, physically or otherwise, bring negativity or destruction to some group or place, question your motive. You get to choose if you will do good or do evil.

For the purposes of getting to the point, I'll assume that you are not planning to take over the world for the purposes of evil. Can we agree on that? Only use the Do Things Method™ for good. Do not use it for evil. Got it? Ok. Moving on.

So, do you remember that epic trip I was telling you about? Let's go back to that. After a surge of inspiration and a week of discussions we decided we would be leaving. Literally, with less than a week of deliberation we were already taking steps towards leaving just over a month later for the entire summer. Everyone we talked with was surprised by our seeming lack of fear to take such a leap of faith. What was there to be afraid of? Worst case scenario, apart from dying on the road, which we acknowledge would be terrible but could just as easily happen crossing the street at home, was that we would have to cut the trip short and come home. Maybe that's reason to have more of a "plan" before we make such a drastic decision, but where's the adventure in that? The adventure is what it's all about, and that is why we did what we did. To live the adventure.

All of that being said, we did need some sort of "plan" before we rumbled off into parts unknown. We needed a little direction. Where should we start? After only a few moments of thought, we said "Let's go east!" That was the extent of our direction. There were a few places that we listed out with intent to visit. Simply a bucket list of locations, we hoped to hit as many as we could before coming home. If we made it, great! If we didn't, there was always the next trip. What? Next trip? Oh, I'm sure there will be a next trip. That was all the "planning" we needed before we started our adventure.

Obviously, when I hit the house our timing changed but did that change our direction? Nope! Simply put, our lack of a plan helped us to adjust after my bonehead actions. If we had reservations, tickets, or anything else that was scheduled we would have been extremely stressed out about getting there in time. Would the RV repairs be done? Was there any additional damage we couldn't see? Could we get refunds on our prepaid plans? None of that even had to be addressed. We could be flexible and roll with the punches as they came. This is by far the greatest advantage of burning your plans...you don't have to scramble and stress when things don't turn out exactly as you expected. Which, in truth, is usually how things turn out.

In the Bible after Moses parted the Red Sea, he and the Israelites wandered in the desert for 40 years before they made it to the promised land. 40 years! They had a direction but no specific plan and eventually, got to where they were meant to be. Yes, they complained and had issues along the way. Mostly caused by their selfish desires, disobedience, and lack of faith in the God that had rescued them from slavery. Did that stop them from ultimately getting to where they were meant to be? No. The small details that go along with that story are great and if you're curious about them, you can read the entire account in the book of Exodus. The big picture in that story is that the Israelites had a direction, stepped out in faith, had issues along the way, and ultimately got to where they were supposed to be. If we look at a huge story like Moses and the Israelites, taking a trip with no step by step plan seems like a no brainer.

In the grand scheme of things, your idea is only going to be as big as it's supposed to be. No amount of planning is going to change that. You are not able to make it bigger or smaller than it is meant to be by having the perfect plan. You may or may not see the gravity of your end goal before you start doing things. As a matter of fact, if you have little to no expectations of what your exact process will be, how much sweeter will it be when you find out? Best surprise EVER! On the flip side, if you spend too much time trying to predict how you will get there, you'll never go anywhere or even worse yet you'll get so upset and distracted when you have to change course that you may stop your journey all together. Things will go wrong. Things will go right. Nothing will go exactly as they are supposed to and that's a good thing. When we are taking steps of faith in the direction of where our vision is leading, enjoying that journey is at least as much of the purpose as getting to the end of it, if not more. Unfortunately, we have a tendency to over focus on details that don't matter and miss what we're experiencing as we go. When we start with just a simple direction instead of a step by step plan dripping with expectations, we don't get paralyzed when we are faced with having to adjust.

For these reasons and many more that can't all be contained in one chapter of one book, you need to burn your plans but hold on to your direction. Get rid of the detailed expectations that will hold you back. Stop worrying about what other people will think. Forget about the things you can't control. Don't obsess about the things that may go wrong...because they probably will. Look at your vision as a simple direction to move. The reason you are doing things. Once you have your perspective clear, you're ready to move onto the next phase of the Do Things Method™. This phase is literally where the title to this method came from. Time for action. Time to starting doing. Time to move towards your goal. Action is the only way to get to where you are meant to be.

Let's DO THINGS.

PHASE 2

PROCESS

CHAPTER 6

LITTLE DRUMMER BOY

As kids, my brother and I loved going over to our grandparents house. They had stairs, a pool, and when our uncle was practicing for a gig, his drums were upstairs. I remember sitting in the room while he practiced the set his swing band would be playing that week. The really cool part about that was, it wasn't just any swing band. Our uncle was a professional drummer. Depending on how old you are, you may or may not recognize the name Lionel Hampton. If you do, great. If you don't, google him. That is who our uncle played with. Our uncle was the real deal.

Whenever my brother and I sat through one of his marathon rehearsals, we would each be wondering, "Will he let us play when he's done?" Sometimes he did. We would sit on that throne and bang the tar out of his finely tuned instrument. At eight and six years old, I assume he knew we couldn't do all THAT much damage. Other times he had to take off for a gig or whatever and we didn't get to. Regardless of whether or not we knew he would let us play, we would still get excited to hear he was at grandma and grandpa's house.

Now, both of our parents were singers, grandpa played the piano, and dad played the trumpet. You could say music was in our blood. Fair enough, but we were never trained in any instruments as kids. We took piano lessons for like five minutes from grandpa but neither my brother or I were ever as excited about that as we were when the drums were around. There's something about taking two sticks of wood, slamming them down on empty shells, and having a rhythmic sound spring forth. Also, it is an excellent excuse to release the crazy energy being held inside of an eight year old boy.

As the years went on, there were only a few instances that we were able to play the drums for an extended amount of time. Then, when we were eleven and nine, our dad came home with one of the most epic surprises ever. When we looked out the window expecting to see dad home from work, he wasn't alone. Our uncle had come over with him. That was strange. Why was our uncle here? Then it happened. They both went back to the trunk to get something. Being curious kids, we came out to see what was going on. As we circled around the back of the car we saw it. NO WAY! It was a full set of Slingerland drums of our very own!

We helped carry the drums inside and quickly got them set up. Uncle Jimmy sat us down, gave us a few pointers, and off we went. Looking back, I'm sure it was not on the top of our dad's list to have his two boys banging on drums all day long. Being a parent now though, I totally understand why that didn't matter. My brother and I would take turns practicing the simple beat our uncle had shown us over, and over, and over. We didn't have plans for what we were doing. We were just doing. We were making it up as we went. It was glorious.

Eventually we mastered the simple beat our uncle had shown us and started creating beats of our own. You need to understand that this was WAY before the days of YouTube. Yes, I'm old. If we wanted to learn a new technique or had trouble with certain sticking patterns we couldn't just look it up. We had to figure it out and that meant a lot of doing. It meant taking action with little to no plans. The only direction we had came from our uncle when the drums were delivered.

Have you ever heard the phrase, "Practice makes perfect?" Well, that's kind of true, but I'd like to change it a bit. Instead of "practice makes perfect" I believe "practice makes progress." Once we start thinking about "perfection" we start to judge ourselves and revert back to those nasty expectations we had when we were creating a step by step plan. Burn that plan! If we can simply look at making "progress" it's much easier to find the encouragement to keep going. If you can master the perspective internally and externally, release control, and have a little direction, our action will create the next step. Essentially when we do things, we let the action guide our process. The process is simple. Do things. Start. Take a step and that step will lead to our next step.

There's a story in the bible that I absolutely love about one of Jesus disciples named Peter. In my opinion, Peter was one of the feistiest followers of Jesus. For some reason, his demeanor speaks to me. Can't imagine why that could be. Anyway, in this particular story all of the disciples are in a boat. While they are on the boat it begins to storm. Now, when I read the story, this is a storm of EPIC proportions. Waves crashing on the deck. Multiple disciples hanging their heads over the side and puking their brains out. As all this is going on, the men see something in the distance coming towards them on the water. Since they're freaking out, and have never seen anyone walk on water before, they assume it's a ghost or some creature coming to take them down. The figure in the distance says it's Jesus. He tells them not to fear and then Peter has a brilliant idea. He's gonna make sure this isn't the Loch Ness Monster pretending to be Jesus. Peter then asks the creature to have him come join him on the water. If you're like me, this logic doesn't really make sense. Why would a grown man think it was a good idea to step out of a perfectly good boat in a storm to see if there is in fact a terrible creature coming to get them or if it is his teacher. Why wouldn't you just wait until the figure was close enough to see for yourself? In any event, the figure tells Peter to come to him. So Peter, in all of his brilliance, steps out of the boat and onto the water. Do you know what happens next? He walks on water. WHAT?!?! It was only for a moment but he did. Peter walked on water.

Jesus asked him to get out of the boat in a circumstance that seemed foolish to pretty much any outsider. All Peter had to go on was a simple direction. He had a seemingly foolish vision. No plan. Not even a literal second step and yet he moved. He did a thing. That thing turned out to be a thing that no man has ever done since and all it took was faith and action. His perspective was clear, and he started a process. It was by faith that he moved, regardless of what others may have thought or said. He listened. He moved. He succeeded.

Most of the time, all we need to do is simply get out of the boat. Listen to the calling you hear, and move. It can be as simple as a step or as grand as a book. Either way, you have to get out of the boat to see what you need to do next. Putting the small pieces together begin to build the big picture. Don't dwell on whether or not you should take the step. That's worse than stressing over every little detail of a plan that you'll never use. Take the step. Hit the drum. Get out of the boat. Start the process. Do the thing. You can't get to where you're meant to go by standing still. Stop being paralyzed by the lack of the perfect plan or by playing the "what if" game about the results you get may or may not get along the way. Once your perspective is clear and you have a direction, it's time to get out of the boat and deal with the results as they come. And they will come.

PHASE 3

RESULTS

CHAPTER 7

SOMETIMES WE SCORE TOUCHDOWNS

Ever since I was little I wanted to be an athlete. My brother and I constantly watched sports, played sports, and imagined what our future sports cards would look like. One of my athletically directed dreams was to play running back and score touchdowns on the gridiron. Unfortunately for me, I was a bigger kid. Typically, the bigger kids don't play running back. In fact, the bigger kids rarely even touch the ball. Now after reading this far, do you think that stopped me from dreaming of being an offensive powerhouse? You guessed it! Not a bit.

When I was a freshman in High School it was time to see what I was made of. It was time for me to play football for the first time. I was a little nervous but ultimately confident in my expected new position as the freshman football running back. On the first day of practice the coaches sat us all down in the bleachers next to the field with the intention of explaining to us how this all worked. When they got to the offensive positions I began to get excited. It was about to be my time to shine.

The coaches walked us through and explained each position choosing individuals from the group to come out and stand in the position they were talking about. After they finished the lineman and quarterback, they got to the running back position. I was sure they would select me to be the example. Why wouldn't they? I was awesome in my own backyard. As the coach called out the running back position, he pointed in my direction. Strangely enough he was slightly off with his aim. It seemed like he was pointing to the smaller, seemingly faster boy sitting next to me. He quickly sprang to his feet and took his place as the running back on the field. What? This wasn't right. How did this happen? At that moment I knew I had a decision. Did I accept my assumed role as something other than a running back or did I refuse to let their perspective change my goal? If you aren't sure how to answer that, I'm guessing you missed the first six chapters of this book. For the rest of you, let's move on!

Over the next few weeks of practice, we were all put to the test. Each of us were evaluated for skill and ability according to our performance during practice. After a week I got my chance. The coaches asked for volunteers to learn the running back position. My hand had never shot up so fast in my life. It was my time. Now they were all gonna see what I already knew to be true. I was the running back. It was me.

It wasn't long before I actually earned the starting running back position. As a matter of fact, I played so well that season that I was selected as the only freshman of our class to move up to Varsity the following year. My sophomore year, I played on the starting defense which was an absolute honor but not the ultimate direction I had envisioned. By my Junior year, I was still on the starting defense but hadn't made my way into the running back position. After the first five weeks, the guy who had been playing running back ahead of me was having issues. His performance wasn't what the coaches had hoped. Was I going to get my shot? Would I be up for the task? We would soon find out.

The week before our sixth game of the season, my coach pulled me aside after practice to tell me that it was going to be me starting that weekend at running back. This was my chance. It was go time. I was pumped out of my mind. When Friday night came, I was calm and confident. This was what I was meant to do...or at least I thought it was.

After the opening kickoff, our defense stopped the other team early and we got the ball back on our own 30 yard line. This would be the first offensive possession of my first varsity game as the starting running back. What was gonna happen? How would this process end up? What was my result going to be? When we got into the huddle, the quarterback called the play. "35 belly, 35 belly. Ready, BREAK!" Wait a minute! That play was a handoff to me! First play was going to me? Let's do this. The ball was snapped and I took the handoff. This play was designed to go off the left side of the line so that's where I started. The offensive lineman and my lead blocker did a great job and I made it past the line of scrimmage, but I didn't stop there. I quickly cut back up field to avoid the defense. Then I saw it.

Three of the other team's players were coming straight for me. Uh-oh! This could get messy. As the defenders got closer, I sped up. Just before all three of the players converged on me to make the tackle, I put my head down to meet them. When we made contact, all three of the defenders flew backwards away from me and fell to the ground. I was still running! I was still moving! No way! By this time, I had gotten about 25 yards down field and after crushing the three opponents that attempted to tackle me, there was only 45 more yards of green grass between me and the endzone. Was this for real? Am I really doing this? Yes I was. The rest of the defense had started to catch up when I collided with the three amigos so I needed to put it into another gear. I pushed my legs to move faster than I had ever moved them before. This was crazy! They weren't catching me. 30...25...20...15...10... TOUCHDOWN! Seriously? That just happened. On my very first play of my very first start as the varsity running back, not only did they give me the ball, but I took that ball, ran over three other human beings then ran away from another eight players to score a 70 yard touchdown! EPIC!

That play set the tone for the rest of the game and we ended up winning after I scored one more touchdown and rushed for close to 200 yards in total. It was a dream come true. It was the night that I had envisioned when I was a little kid. There were many other games, touchdowns, victories, losses, fumbles, and tackles but that night will forever be ingrained in my memory. Why? Why will I never forget that night? Well, first of all because it was EPIC and I still have the video to remind me. It's on my Instagram page and YouTube if you're interested. But maybe even more importantly, it made an impact on my life in a way that wouldn't have happened had I never taken that handoff. The result from that process, that action, that thing I did, gave me opportunities.

After High School, I received a scholarship to play Division 1 college football and eventually it brought me to where I am right now, writing this book to share these stories with you. This story is meant to illustrate to you that doing something as simple as taking a handoff can sometimes give you the exact result you're looking for. Sometimes, you succeed on the first try. It happens. Did you know that? It's true. However, we usually live in the negative land of "what if it goes bad?" instead of thinking, "what if it succeeds?" We look back at all the stuff that didn't go as planned and assume that we will never succeed or perhaps even worse, look back and think it can never get any better.

Think of it this way, if I had never decided to attempt playing football, I would've never scored that first varsity touchdown. If Noah had never started cutting down trees to build a boat that, at the time, was a work of fantasy, he would've never survived a flood. If Moses had never raised his staff at the Red Sea, the Israelites would have never escaped the Egyptian army. If David had never put those stones in his pocket, he never would have defeated Goliath. If Peter had never stepped out of the boat, he would have never walked on water. My point is, you can't get amazing results if you never do things. You have to take action, even though it may not turn out the way you expected and when it does, you have to be willing to humble yourself and reevaluate your approach to whatever it is you're trying to accomplish. Because we don't always score a touchdown. Not even close. Sometimes a student lights a firecracker during class.

CHAPTER 8

SOMETIMES STUDENTS LIGHT FIRECRACKERS DURING CLASS

Ok, so I admit the last chapter ended with an exceptionally dramatic cliffhanger. Yes, it was an attempt to get you intrigued about this next chapter. If we think about it, we've all had some similar incident that caught our attention like the shocking sound of a firecracker being set off in the middle of a silent class. It steals our attention and ultimately causes us to recognize some major flaw in our current process. Do you want to know a secret? That actually happened to me. Let me tell you about it.

It was the spring of 2004 and I was in my final semester of college. As I was going through school and the time came for me to select a focus for my major, there was a lot to consider. What did I know? What did I like to do? Where did I want to be? How could I do as little work as possible but still make a decent living? While all of these questions were bouncing around in my head, I thought back over my time in high school and how great it was being on campus, scoring touchdowns on Friday nights, and interacting with my friends every day. "How great would it be to just do that again?" I thought. The more I thought, the more it started to make sense, "Wait a minute, why COULDN'T I do that again? I'll just be a teacher and coach sports." It made so much sense to me. All of my coaches from the past seemed to enjoy their jobs. Thinking of where I would be, what I would do, and how it would work it just seemed like the logical decision. So it was decided, I was going to be a high school Teacher and Coach.

Now that I was in my final semester of college, it was time to take a little teaching test drive of sorts. It was time for student teaching. When I arrived at the school I was assigned to, it was simple to introduce myself. "Hi, my name is Mr. Frazier and I play Division 1 football at the local college. Who likes sports?" I was a hit. The kids really enjoyed me being in class and the teacher...well I think the teacher enjoyed me. She always gave me positive reviews and told me how great I was doing. Maybe that's just what they tell every student teacher to keep their confidence up so they make it into the program. Either way, it seemed like I was on the road to success in the educational field.

On the last week of my eight week student teaching experience, I was given the class all to myself to instruct so I could get a real feel for what I was about to get myself into. "Sweet! This will be a piece of cake," I thought to myself. Just as I expected, the first few days of the week were great. We covered most of the material, told jokes, had some laughs, and mainly just enjoyed hanging out together. The last day of my week, we were scheduled to have a small class party to celebrate the year and say goodbye to me as their student teacher. It seemed like it was the perfect way to end my student teaching and prepare to jump into my future profession. In the third period of the day I was giving my short lecture portion to the class about using some formula to solve an equation. I really don't remember what I was talking about because what happened next changed my entire life and caused me to forget the details of that morning.

My back was turned to the students as I was demonstrating the formula on the board. "Ok, so you will take this value and substitute the "x" with...." BANG! There was the loudest noise I'd ever heard in a classroom that exact instant. It was an explosion. It smelled like gunpowder but as I quickly swirled around to see what had happened there was no gun present and all the students were staring towards the back of the class at a single student. Now, this was before the days when school shootings were as common as they seem to be in 2018. It's a sad truth in our society today and it makes me hurt for students that have been affected by violence in the classroom. This sound however was not from a gun. No, it was an explosion for sure, but not a gunshot.

I slowly walked towards the back of the room with I'm sure the most confused and dumbfounded expression on my face. When I got to the student that the rest of the class was staring at, he had the most epic grin on his face. "Dude, what was that?" I asked in disbelief as he continued to smile.

"What, this? Oh, it was a firecracker." the student replied as if this was a common occurrence in every class across the country.

"What?!?! You can't light a firecracker off during class! You gotta go to the principal's office." As I told this to the student, he looked at me with confusion and concern about my ability to understand what he had just done. After we stared at each other for which seemed like 45 minutes but I'm sure was only a few seconds he said, "What? Why? I thought you were a cool teacher?" That was not what I expected him to say.

As I attempted to explain to him that it didn't matter how cool I was, that was not something a student should ever do in a classroom, it hit me like a ton of bricks. "What am I doing?" I thought. At that moment, my entire student teaching career flashed before my eyes. Remember how I said we got through MOST of the material but basically just had a good time? Yeah, that was how I was teaching. Like I was just another student having a good time. I then realized that my ability to handle a classroom full of adolescents on a daily basis may not be the best use of my skills. For some reason, the way I had conducted myself gave at least one student the feeling that he could do whatever he wanted because I would be "cool" about it. This was not going to work for me.

As I drove home that night in a silent car thinking over the events that took place, it became incredibly clear that my process was in jeopardy. My expectations of what being a teacher was like needed some serious adjustments. It was time to adjust or change. Those were the only two options I could see. Could I spend the rest of my life wondering if my classroom management skills were up to par? Was I willing to change my style to use more discipline tactics and sacrifice some of my ability to relate to the students in the way that felt most natural? The questions continued to come into my brain as I drove into the parking lot of our apartment building.

When I walked in the door I told Tammy what had happened. Since we were already married and had started to make plans for our future with me as an educator, I had to explain that we may need to change our direction. My skill set didn't seem to map to being a teacher like I had thought. Really, my perspective about what it meant to be a teacher wasn't what I thought it was.

It was critical that I looked at this incident with humility to see what I had done wrong. Sure, the student that went too far had responsibility in that moment as well but remember, you can't control Christmas...or your student's actions. At that moment, I decided to see this "failure" as a building block to my next step...whatever it would end up being. I needed to burn those plans

Recognizing my faults, or rather my lack of skill and desire to continue on the road of being a teacher was critical to me getting where I am today. Looking back, I am so thankful that some student lit a firecracker during my class. It was the smack across the face I needed to wake up and realize that I wasn't suited for life in a classroom. What is it going to take for you to realize you aren't a fit for the direction you're going? You have to be honest and humble when you think about that. We can easily hide behind a fake confidence or blame outside factors for our downfall. The reality is that we always have some ownership in anything good or bad that happens. Once we realize that, we can focus on the things we can change and make an adjustment or two before we start the process again because it doesn't end with defeat or loss. Nope. That's just another part of the process. An extremely important part of the process.

There's a parable that Jesus tells in the Bible about a father and a son. If you don't know, a parable is a story that is told with the sole intent of giving a word picture that further illustrates some specific or multiple specific points to be interpreted by the listener. Jesus used these a lot. So in this story that is commonly referred to as the prodigal son, Jesus talks of a wealthy father and his two sons. The younger son requests his part of the inheritance early so he can go out and enjoy it as he pleases. The father agrees and the son takes off to parts unknown. You may think this boy to be foolish. From our perspective, you would be correct. From that boy's perspective, he had a vision and direction of what he wanted for his life and he decided to take action. As he goes about his journey, things start off great. He has parties, hangs out with friends, and lives what I'm sure he expected to be the adventure he was meant to live. The story continues and very soon he is out of money, his friends are gone, and he has nothing left. At this point, he realizes that he has made a grave mistake.

With no other alternative in sight, he swallows his pride, gathers up as much humility as possible, and goes back to the father hoping that he'll be accepted back home even though his father may not allow him in. Remember, you can't control Christmas, but you can always make a list. When he returns, his father is ecstatic and welcomes him in with open arms. This story says so many different things all at once. If you read the story for yourself, there is even more to unpack, but for the purposes of this chapter, we will focus on the younger son. The son needed a smack across the face to make him realize he needed to change his direction. He thought he was going in the right direction. The direction he wanted to go. The direction that ultimately led him to realize, in humility, that he needed to change his direction.

The parable of the prodigal son is a powerful one. As I mentioned, it tells multiple stories all at the same time. The one thing we need to make sure to realize about this story when we view it through the eyes of the younger son, is this: this story is not intended to give us justification to take intentionally destructive or harmful selfish direction. Yes, we will all make mistakes and may need a wakeup call to realize the error in our direction. However, when we choose a direction, we need to remember to start from the perspective that we are a MIRACLE created to do AMAZING things. If the direction we are heading has obvious and unavoidable reasons not to proceed because harm will come to you or others around you, it's time to stop and re-evaluate what your purpose is. Remember, the Do Things Method™ is intended for good and NOT evil.

That being said, we all have a unique perspective. In that understanding, we need to realize that each of us has an opportunity to do a thing that may or may not work out. Just because you see something as foolish, doesn't mean that it is. It also means that it might be. Regardless of whether you are right or wrong, you have to decide to take action or to change direction. So many times we sit in limbo trying to decide if our theory about what result we may or may not get by taking a certain action and never actually move. The "plan" we devise many times stops us from moving for fear of failure or even just being a little bit wrong. That's where the problem is. We never act. We never move. We never actually get a result to know for a fact if our theory was right or wrong. In my experience, the best way to decide about changing direction is with the results you receive after you make a move. It's either a touchdown or a firecracker or maybe something in between. With that result, you have to make another decision, "Do I keep going the same way?", "Do I adjust my direction slightly?" or, "We've got to turn this bus around!" That takes us to the final phase of the Do Things Method™. Time to repeat.

PHASE 4

REPEAT

CHAPTER 9

PUPPIES AND THE CPA EXAM

If you didn't get enough about puppies at Christmas from my earlier story, you're in luck! As I told you, I have a family of five. There's me, my wife, and our three children. Our oldest daughter seems to be similar to her old dad when it comes to lists for Christmas, although she had a much better tactic than I did.

When our oldest was four years old, she wanted a puppy. She wanted a puppy for Christmas. In fact, all she wanted for Christmas was a puppy. See, she was much smarter than her dad making the infinite Christmas list. Her list consisted of one thing. A puppy. As a father, especially one that had loved puppies before, I knew it was a slam dunk that she would get one on Christmas morning.

On Christmas morning that year, her mom and I went into her room to tell her she could come downstairs to see what was under the tree. Her eyes were wide with anticipation and she had a smile so big that it lit up the entire house. Her brother and sister were too young to join in the anticipation but they caught on soon enough and ran down the stairs with smiles on their faces. Just as her uncle and I had raced to the tree when we were young, she sped down the stairs and around the corner so fast that her minnie mouse nightgown could barely keep up.

There it was. A ginormous red box with a huge bow that seemed to be making noises. She stood in front of the box jumping up and down with her hands clasped together repeating "My puppy, my puppy, my puppy…" over and over and over. When the rest of us caught up to her and gathered around the box we told her she could take off the lid. She bent down and gently removed the top of the box revealing the scruffy blond puppy hidden inside. It felt like she was so excited her head might actually explode. To be honest, I think I was so excited that my head almost exploded. Luckily, there were no explosions of any type that morning. She got a puppy. She loved her puppy. That was a given. Only one question remained, would the puppy love her?

As she stared down at her perfect little puppy, we heard a sound coming from the fluffy bundle of joy. It wasn't the kind of sound any of us had expected to hear. The puppy seemed to be growling! What? This was supposed to be the perfect Christmas morning puppy that would leap out of the box into her arms, wag its tail, and lick her face while she giggled uncontrollably all morning long. That is not how it unfolded.

All five of us stared down at the puppy with confusion as we listened to the low hum of his seemingly unhappy tone. Our daughter looked at us as if to say, "Mom, Dad, what do I do?" Tammy and I looked back at her and told her to reach down slowly to pet him and speak softly so he feels comfortable. She nodded with a look of determination, turned back to the puppy, and began her descent to the great box of wonder. The closer she got, the lowder the puppy's growl got. She backed off, then tried again. Same result. What was missing?

Her perspective was spot on. She was a miracle, the puppy was a miracle, Christmas was a miracle, and she wasn't letting mean Christmas box puppy keep her from creating the most special relationship any child ever had with a Christmas puppy. Her process had started. She reached down slowly and gently. When that result didn't work out as she had hoped, she tried again, and again. She was in the repeat stage of the Do Things Method™.

Now we had to decide if it was time to keep going with our current process, make a small adjustment to the direction, or turn the bus around completely. Hopefully by now you can guess which path we took. My wife had a great adjustment to our process. She quickly went into the kitchen to grab something out of the fridge. My daughter and I looked at each other puzzled at how mommy was going to help while she took a snack break.

Before we could even process what she could possibly be getting she had returned. In her hand was a pile of juicy turkey lunch meat. Yes! How do you control the urges of a wild animal, husband or child? By giving them something to eat. It was brilliant. She gave our daughter a small piece of the meat and explained how she should approach the puppy slowly but instead of petting him, she should stick her fingers in his mouth with a tasty treat. Wait. That sounds dangerous. It was fine. Our daughter was tough.

She gave a confident nod, grabbed the turkey in her cute little balled up fist, and set out to convince this puppy that he loved her. As she approached this time with a tasty treat in her outstretched grasp, the puppy stopped growling and tilted his head to the side as she got closer. "It's ok puppy, I'm not a monster." This was how our daughter assumed the little puppy saw her, as a monster. However, she knew that she was a sweet girl that just wanted to love her new pet. She got closer and closer until finally she was able to give the puppy a tasty treat. His tail started to wag, but he was still hesitant to embrace his new friend. She gave him another treat and still another. Each time she moved a little closer until finally she had knelt down right in front of the box nose to nose with her new best friend. The two locked eyes for just a moment and then it happened. The puppy put his paws up on the side of the box as a sign of approval. We lifted him out and put him in our daughter's arms. She did it! It was a touchdown. From that day on, her little pal was by her side. They were true friends all because, instead of quitting after she didn't get the result she had hoped for, we adjusted the direction just slightly, and started again.

The results are not the end. The results of any process are just a measurement of how the process needs to either be maintained or adjusted. If we stop every time we get negative results, we'd never actually accomplish anything. Actually, if we quit every time something negative happened, we may be better off pontificating about a lengthy, intricate plan that we never take action on. At least then we would still get to dream about the what ifs, even though our plan would keep us from ever getting anywhere. Does that make sense? Let's try one more story.

So after the firecracker incident caused me to derail my plans to be in education, I got an offer to enter real estate investing. It was a great job and I did very well. After just two years I had gotten my real estate brokers license and was managing over $18,000,000 of real estate investments. Unfortunately, in 2008 the real estate market took a dive and I lost my job. What would I do? How would I support my family of five? Something needed to happen fast. The one thing that I had always thought could be a possible career choice was the only option that spoke to me. My father had been a CPA for over 20 years and owned his own firm. I figured I could ask him for an opportunity to work for him as an entry level employee while I prepared to take the exam required to be a licensed CPA myself and then start my own practice. After all, what's the worst that could happen? I was already unemployed.

When I asked my dad about working for him, he agreed and said it would be great to work with his son. Perfect! I took a chance and got to take another step. One down, 5,000,000 to go. The situation was this: first, my pay would be half of what I was making at my previous job. Second, because I was an education major in college, I had over 60 additional credits I needed to get by going back to college during my off hours. Last, I had to study to take the four part CPA exam that has been called the second hardest exam, next to the bar exam for attorneys. Did I mention my wife and three young children? No big deal, I would just start with a direction and do things. Right?

Over the next six years I would work full time for my father, go to class at night and online to get the required education to qualify to take the CPA exam, try to spend time with my growing family, and hope I didn't die from lack of sleep. No problem. One step at a time.

After I finally got all of the education out of the way, all I had to do was pass this exam. It was a four part exam and when you pass one section you get 12 months to pass the other three before that result expires and you have to retake the section. Yeah, not gonna lie, that was stressful just thinking about it. Amongst figuring out how to study and scheduling exams I finally was able to attempt my first section.

When I finished taking the exam I felt alright. Not great, not bad, just alright. As I waited for the results of this first section, I immediately started studying for the next section. Two weeks passed and I got my result. It was a 26. Not like 26 out of 30 or 26 out of 40, it was a 26 percent. Oh yeah. This was bad. I had to receive an 85 or higher on each section to pass. What had I gotten myself into? As I continued to attempt exams, my results stayed pretty low. The results were consistent and I didn't pass any section the first try, so I adjusted some of my study habits and attempted again. Failed all four again. Made a few more adjustments to my studying, failed a few more sections. This was getting ridiculous. Maybe my perspective was off. When we talked with friends and family about what was happening we usually got asked if we were doing the right thing. We would go home, I would evaluate my results, think through their comments, review my vision and still feel confident that this was what I was supposed to be doing. Either I was going to learn a lesson about "not listening to reason" or "how perseverance wins the race". I chose to believe it was the perseverance lesson. So I kept going.

In all, I had to take three sections of the CPA exam six times and one section eight times. That is a total of 26 times I went to a testing site, sat down at a computer, and attempted to pass this exam. If you do the math, my success rate was an abysmal 15%. You know what? It was all worth it. The discipline and self motivation it taught both me and my wife were life changing. After passing the exam I started my own practice and within six months had earned over $100,000. Crazy! My first business was an overnight success. An eight year, no sleep, constant grind, overnight success! Did you pick up on my sarcasm there? They don't have a sarcasm font and I usually use emojis when I write sarcasm online so I'm hoping that "overnight success" bit made sense.

It was NOT an overnight success. It took a lot of perspective, a ton of process, and consistent results with endless repetition to get it right. Just because you don't get the result you hoped for on your first attempt, doesn't mean you stop. It means you start back at the top, evaluate your perspective and process, make necessary adjustments and go again. You have to be confident in your direction and patient in your process.

There is a story about a guy named Joshua in the Bible that took over leading the Israelites after Moses died. The particular story that speaks to this part of the Do Things Method™ has to do with a city named Jericho. Now, God had promised these great lands to his people but they would need to conquer existing cities to take control of the territories. When they came to the city of Jericho, Joshua got a direction from God that they were to march around the city walls, blow trumpets and the walls would come down. Wait, what? That can't be serious. Yep, they marched around the walls for seven days waiting for the walls to crumble. This may be crazier than taking the CPA exam over and over. In the story, on the seventh day they were to march around the city seven times and after the seventh time, the priests would blow the trumpets and the walls would fall. I have to believe that after the third day of this, the people of Jericho all climbed to the top of the wall to watch in amazement that these people were just walking around. I'm sure there were more than a few "mean internet ladies" that talked about how they were horrible for drinking their least favorite coffee. That didn't stop them. They kept on course and ultimately defeated the city and took control of the land that God had set out for them.

If we keep a 10,000 foot view of what we're trying to do, we don't get held down by the details that usually change when we start the process anyway. Staying focused on the big picture allows us to see that it is going to take a process with constant adjustments and seemingly endless repetition if we really want to get to living the life we are meant to live. It's not complicated, but it can be difficult because it takes effort. It takes action. The plan doesn't get you closer. The plan doesn't get you results. It's the action and consistency that gets us there. In the best of scenarios, the process itself is one of the best parts of the ride. After all, if we are going to have to repeat something over and over, we might as well enjoy that adventure too!

CHAPTER 10

FROM SPEAKING TO CELEBRITIES

The real catalysts for me attempting to write this book is that over the past year I have been given multiple opportunities to speak on stage in front of thousands of people to share my stories, insight, and encouragement. In fact, my original intent was not to write an entire book. My intent was to create a simple pamphlet or detailed outline to share with people at events where I speak. As it has evolved into what it is now, I've been following the Do Things Method™ every step of the way. This has all been a process and it's all connected. Let me show you.

The first major opportunity to speak came at my church when I was asked to speak at our summer Vacation Bible School for the kids from Kindergarten through fifth grade. It didn't seem like too difficult of a task so I agreed to take the opportunity. The leadership told me there would be over 1,500 kids and adult leaders there for five days in a row to hear me speak for 20 minutes each day. A few important details that I have yet to mention is that I had never spoken for two days in a row, let alone five, and never to more than a hundred people. It may have seemed crazy from the outside, but something about this just felt right.

The week came, I spoke, they listened (as well as kindergarten through fifth grade children listen), and we all survived. After that week, my focus shifted from that being a one time opportunity, to thinking that this may be something that I had a gift to do. What would it look like if I was to pursue being a public speaker? How would I do it? What would I talk about? Who would I talk to? Those and many other questions flashed through my mind. With no real rhyme or reason I took to the place where I tend to get the most instant feedback, the internet! Without hesitation I opened my Facebook account and typed this:

"Hey everyone! So I'm thinking about doing some public speaking. Does anyone have an idea where I should start?"

It wasn't more than a few hours before I started receiving quite a bit of feedback but one message in particular caught my attention. It was my friend that happened to be the principal at a local Jr. High. He said they were having a first week of school kick-off assembly and asked if I would want to start there. Whoa! Crazy. If that wasn't a sign that I was onto something, I don't know what is.

We messaged a few times and it was done. I was scheduled to be the first day of school speaker at a local Jr. High. Oh, and it was a paid opportunity. They were paying me $500 to stand in front of the kids and talk into a microphone. This was too awesome. But what would I talk about? I couldn't use the messages I gave at church earlier that summer. It needed to be a general message that I could share across many speaking engagements. I needed a catch phrase. I needed a brand. As I thought over the stories I could tell and how they all related to each other the message became clear. My message was that people need to DO THINGS. Every time I ran through a story from my past, it was all about taking action even though the plan wasn't fully formed. That was it! On that day, DO THINGS was born.

That engagement came, I spoke, they listened, and my desire to speak grew. Unbeknownst to me, my ability to share a message from stage had been shared through the grapevine and my friend who had invited me to speak at his school shared that he had been contacted by an executive from a statewide organization that put on events for students in leadership. They inquired about my message and if they could get in touch with me. This, again was confirmation to me that my direction was true.

Over the next few weeks the organization contacted me and invited me to come speak to thousands of Jr High and High School students in San Diego about Doing Things. I agreed and began to prepare. As my message became more and more defined, I thought it might be cool to have something that I wore as a signature representing my brand. Since I wasn't a "dress up" kind of guy, I started thinking about designing a custom t-shirt to wear when I was speaking. I jumped on my computer and started trying to design a simple logo to put on a shirt. You need to know that I have no design experience and had never made any custom clothes before. When I was done, it was just a simple rectangle with the words "DO THINGS" across the middle. Worked for me.

Since the event was coming up in the next few days, I didn't have time to figure out some lavish online custom t-shirt situation because it wouldn't get to me in time. In lieu of that, I used an iron-on option to make a homemade custom t-shirt. It wasn't perfect, but it was a shirt and it had my brand on it. That week I wore it to the event and surprisingly got a few comments about it. The event went well and I have been asked to speak many more times for this organization. The thing that was interesting about this event was that I tried something new and it worked. I created a custom t-shirt that people seemed to react to. That made me start to think about what other things could be done with clothing. Back to the internet!

It wasn't long before I had found a way to create more designs on multiple types of apparel and created a website to be ready to sell these products if at my next event anyone was interested. Wait, I had an idea, did a little research, took some action and now I have an apparel website to accompany my speaking business. Do you see how fluid that was? If you are paying attention to what's happening around you, opportunities will present themselves and all you have to do is take a little action and so much can happen...but this isn't the end of that story.

As I built the products and started wearing only apparel I created, the idea and my vision for what this would become grew larger and larger. This was bigger than just something for me to connect when I was speaking to groups. I was building a real brand that had a message to help people take action and live the adventure they were meant to live. So now I had to figure out a way to get more exposure for what I was building.

One night, my family and I were on the couch watching our favorite show Survivor. If you've never seen it, you really should start. It's easily my favorite show and it could be yours too. Anyway, it was the finale and one of the cast members that we really liked ended up getting voted out and didn't win. He was on stage during the finale and what he said gave me an idea. He said he wanted to be a positive role model and help people. Well that sounded like a Do Things attitude if I'd ever heard one. That instant, I took to social media. Earlier in the season I had messaged him a few times on Instagram so we had a small relationship already. My message to him was simple. I told him I had an apparel business and wondered if he'd like to be involved.

The next day he messaged me back. His response was simple.

"That sounds great! Let's talk more."

We messaged back and forth a few more times and eventually met for coffee. Over the next few weeks we talked ideas, designs, and Survivor. Eventually we decided to create his very own brand of apparel and put it together with my apparel to build an apparel company to reach other online influencers and possible build their brands as well. The business is still in its infancy, but it exists, and we're super pumped about it.

The reason I tell you that story is to illustrate that the Do Things Method™ is a process that can take you anywhere and everywhere if you're patient and alert. If I had never decided to try speaking at my church, I would never have started an apparel brand and met a celebrity who I have become friends and business partners with. As a matter of fact, it was him and his girlfriend that were the couple my wife and I were talking with before we decided to take our epic 86 day, 43 states, and Canada RV adventure. It's all connected. It's all a process. It's the Do Things Method™.

CHAPTER 11

SO, NOW WHAT?

Congratulations! You've finished...or did you? At this point, you probably feel one of a few different ways. Some of you may feel like there is nothing that can stop you! You're ready to start doing things. Some of you may still be worried about what your version of "Mean Internet Lady" will say if you start moving. You may also think that all you've learned about the Do Things Method™ is fine and dandy, but it's still too hard for you to get up and take action. To all of you I say, exactly.

Exactly! Each and every one of us will have a different feeling after learning the Do Things Method™. As a matter of fact, that is expected. Because of that, I want to tell you something. You are not alone. It's true! You are not the only one. Countless others across the globe will have issues and setbacks. Reasons not to start. Reasons to stop going. Yes, even those that feel like they are ready to run through a brick wall after reading this will stumble and fall. That is why it doesn't end here. It can't end here. You are a MIRACLE created to do AMAZING things and so is the person next to you, across from you, and around the corner from you. We are all in this together. It is true that the only things we have control over is our perspective and effort. However, the best way to implement the Do Things Method™ is by leaning on the support and encouragement of a community you can trust to keep you going. That is what you do now. It's time to join together and make things happen.

Even before you've established your perspective; before you accept that you are a MIRACLE; before you block out Mean Internet Lady, and you see the direction you are headed; before you even start the process, we want to join you! What ever your journey is, let us come with you. If you're interested, you might be thinking, "Great! I'd love that...but how do we get in touch?" Let me tell you.

If you want to join the Do Things Community and get support and encouragement in all phases of the Do Things Method™, here is what we are going to do. First, you can join our closed Facebook group called "The Do Things Community". Simply search "The Do Things Community" or "Burn Your Plans" on Facebook and request to join the group! I'll be there along with others that share your desire to take action. In addition, if you want to share your journey in a more public forum, that would be AMAZING! You can use the hashtags #DoThingsMethod or #BurnYourPlans on every social network and we will join with you!

Also, if you have a group that would benefit from hearing about the Do Things Method™ and why they should burn their plans live and in person, I would love to come share at your next event! Having an in person opportunity to share our struggles and successes enhances any bond. When we get together, share our perspective, and discuss how to overcome together, there is nothing that can stop us.

It's really simple: get the perspective, start the process, get a result, and then repeat. You can do it. We want to help. This is the time. This is the year! I know you will have setbacks but don't let that stop you. Join the community, stay on track, and BURN THOSE PLANS!

Facebook.com/groups/BurnYourPlans

#DoThingsMethod   #BurnYourPlans

For LIVE bookings: Todd@FrazierMethod.com

THE END...UNTIL YOU START AGAIN

1. INTERNAL

    o   YOU are a MIRACLE

2. EXTERNAL

    o   Mean Internet Lady
    o   Haters gonna Hate

3. YOU CAN'T CONTROL CHRISTMAS

    o   All you have is perspective and effort

4. DIRECTION

    o   Let's go east!

PROCESS

1. DO THINGS!

RESULTS

1. WHAT WAS A TOUCHDOWN?
2. WHAT WAS A FIRECRACKER?
3. WHAT CAN YOU ADJUST?

REPEAT

1. START THE PROCESS AGAIN

NOTES: